I0154906

COMBAT
WITHOUT
WEAPONS

COMBAT WITHOUT WEAPONS

by

Lt. E. HARTLEY LEATHER R.C.A.

The Naval & Military Press Ltd

Published by

The Naval & Military Press Ltd

Unit 5 Riverside, Brambleside
Bellbrook Industrial Estate
Uckfield, East Sussex
TN22 1QQ England

Tel: +44 (0)1825 749494

www.naval-military-press.com
www.nmarchive.com

*In reprinting in facsimile from the original, any imperfections are inevitably
reproduced and the quality may fall short of modern type and cartographic standards.*

This book is published strictly for historical purposes.

The Naval and Military Press Ltd expressly bears no responsibility or liability of any type, to any first, second or third party, for any harm, injury or loss whatsoever.

PREFACE

A SIMPLE handbook of the subject, prepared not for the professional wrestler but for the average Home Guardsman with no special training and a minimum of time to master the subject, this little book is dedicated specially to those middle-aged men who have rallied to the defence of their country, their homes, and their families; and is written in such a way as to be readily put into practice regardless of a man's physical condition. It suggests not only the physical steps to be taken in dealing hand to hand with the Nazi, but, even more important, the mental attitude of ruthlessness, which amounts simply to victory at all costs—the only outlook which will ever get us out of our present predicament.

CONTENTS

ACKNOWLEDGMENTS

My sincere gratitude to all the members of my staff for their guidance and co-operation in preparing this pamphlet. In particular to Sergt.-Instructor J. D. Kane and Sergt.-Instructor E. A. Harsant for their good-spirited rough-and-tumble in making the illustrations for this book. Also to Messrs. Gale & Polden, Ltd., my publishers, for their many helpful suggestions and for giving me the opportunity of putting this knowledge before the public.

E. H. C. L.

England.
January, 1942.

THE AUTHOR

LIEUTENANT E. HARTLEY LEATHER
ROYAL CANADIAN ARTILLERY

AUTHOR'S NOTE

I TAKE this opportunity to express my thanks to those Home
Guard Commanders to whom I have already lectured, as they
are really responsible for the present writing. To those many
other battalions and companies I have not visited may I
express the wish that you will derive some benefit from my
work, and also add that if you should wish to communicate
with me with the intention of a personal demonstration I
shall be only too happy to comply?

COMBAT WITHOUT WEAPONS

INTRODUCTION

THIS little book is written with just two objects in view—brevity and simplicity. There are numerous texts on the subject, which is really a simplified version of the well-known jiu-jitsu. Unfortunately, most people still find it rather complicated and involved, and in this short volume we will try to reduce it to its lowest common denominator. Our idea is not to attempt to make specialists out of average people, but simply to teach a few simple tricks that everyone can learn in a matter of minutes, that will make you more efficient at the task we all have to hand—exterminating Germans.

The phrase " exterminating Germans " is used purposely, because we must always remember that *all* Germans live for just one purpose, and that is exterminating *all* Englishmen; and therefore the only hope of winning this war is in our doing the job first. Every honest man must believe that to-day, and if he does not believe it he is not an honest man.

No matter how unsavoury the job may be, it has got to be done, and done thoroughly; remember, the German is always thorough: we will only beat him if we play his own game, because he will never play ours. Sportsmanship and decency are entirely foreign to his nature. Kicking a man when he is down does not appeal to the average Briton, but we must forget our long-learned niceties when dealing with the Boche; the Nazi is congenitally incapable of being decent. It is not a matter solely of beating the Hun; it is even more than that—a matter of saving your own life and those of your wife and your children.

"SMASH HIS HEAD ON THE GROUND"

RUTHLESSNESS

Ruthlessness can best be defined in two words—speed and brutality. Your gentlemanly qualities will no doubt be offended by much of the following, but if you do not take it to heart you may be sure that at some future date your own neck will be a good deal more offended. In personal combat, as much as in the strategy of armies, the two chief elements of success are surprise and speed. It does not matter twopence what you do so long as you do it fast, and when you do it, do it as though your life depended on it, because it probably does.

Always realize that the Nazi expects this kind of treatment, and he is quite prepared to use it on you. If you have a streak of hate in you now is the time to let it out; and don't just let it out—let it run riot! When you meet the Boche in your own High Street, if you feel most of all like hitting him on the jaw, then by all means do so. But do not hit him with the intention of knocking him out: break his jaw. **A fractured jaw takes months to heal and is extraordinarily painful: it will give him plenty of time to think about all those Polish women he raped and murdered in 1939!** If you think of them just before you hit him you will be amazed by the sting you can put into your punch! A good rugger tackle is also highly effective if properly done; but, once again, **do not tackle him with the idea of knocking him off his feet: crack his skull on the pavement!** If you should make the mistake of going to the ground with him, do not waste time hitting him or trying to throttle him. **Smash his head on the ground!** It may seem strange at first, but after all that is the object you are aiming at. Never strike an unnecessary blow. Mr. Churchill has boundless energy, but the rest of us have none to spare. Do not waste it; **make every blow count, every attack fatal.**

"A GOOD BASH IN THE NOSE"

THE STEEL HELMET

The steel helmet was originally designed by some optimist as a protection against shell splinters and small-arms fire. Whether it is or not is rather a debatable point, but what most people do not realize is that it is a first-class weapon of offence, and in fact in really close work it is the last line of attack. One of the first principles of street fighting is **keep your man at arm's length,** where you can get at him and see what he is up to. But if he should get in close, grasp you around the waist, for instance, a good bash in the nose with the sharp edge of the helmet will soon make him let go. In order to make this even more effective, you might sharpen the edge of the rim with a file!

Many books illustrate some very effective releases from grips around the waist, under the arms; but after all no one but an absolute fool would ever grasp a man and leave both his arms free. If anyone does, he will get just what he deserves—a good right hook to the jaw. Do not confuse your mind with non-essentials—**get the fundamentals and get going!**

By the same token, if you should ever close with a man in this fashion—and don't say we did not warn you not to —keep your head down, duck your chin right into your shoulder.

Now someone will ask, " Supposing your opponent has learnt this trick also? " Well, kick him in the shins: his head will come up!

Do not think, however, that a bash on the face with the helmet is an end in itself; that only makes your opponent loosen up. Never half do a job. Once he has slackened off crack him in the jaw with your fist, or smash your knee into his crotch. Or, better still, do both!

11

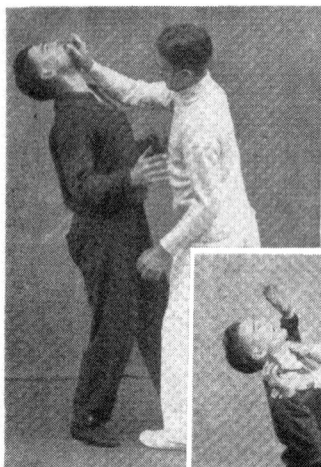

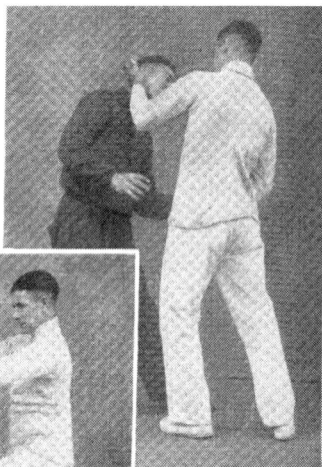

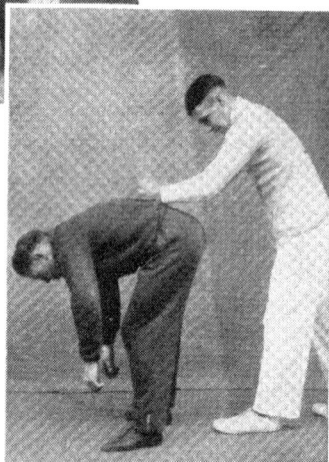

THE VULNERABLE POINTS ON A MAN'S BODY

VULNERABLE POINTS

A man's body is made up of many parts. Some are soft, some are hard. Some bend, some do not. In some places nerves are near the surface; in others they are not. Note these few points in the accompanying plates, and see how each may best be attacked.

Chin.—If you are handy with your fists nothing can beat a good, solid punch on the jaw. A heel-of-the-hand punch also packs a terrific "wallop," and is much easier for those not experienced in the "gentle art."

Windpipe.—A rabbit punch across the windpipe causes temporary black-out. While your man is in this dazed condition, finish him off—blow to the jaw, knee to the crotch, arm lock: what you will.

Sides of the Throat.—A well-delivered rabbit punch just under the ears will at least dislocate the neck, and very probably break it.

Crotch.—Probably the most vulnerable and sensitive part of the body. A knee or foot in the proper place from the weakest man will knock the strongest man senseless.

Kidneys and Small of Back.—The main nerve and muscle cords of the body branch out like a tree from the base of the spine, and at this point are very near to the surface. A two-fisted punch here has a great stunning effect. If delivered quickly a man cannot even cry out.

Knees.—When stalking a man from behind a kick in the back of the knee will make him "fold up," and give you a much better target for finishing the job efficiently.

Arms.—There are three joints in the arm—the wrist, elbow and shoulder. They are all designed to bend one way and one way only. If you force them the other way they must either break or your man goes down. The choice is up to him, and it is immaterial to you.

Also note from these plates that there are three good ways of punching—the fist, the rabbit punch, and the heel-of-the-hand punch. The last two, although not so widely known, are very effective. A heel of the hand in the jaw snaps the head back and may very easily break the neck. A rabbit punch on the soft part of the neck or base of the skull may be equally disconcerting for your opponent, and do just as much damage. Their beauty is in their simplicity. A man not used to using his fists may very easily dislocate a finger or break a thumb if he is not very careful.

13

THE KICK

An ordinary straight kick is a narrow object aimed at a narrow target, and the slightest move on your opponent's part may cause you to miss, leaving you wide open for his attentions. Kick him with the inside of the foot and aim at a point about a foot behind his instep. Make contact a few inches below the knee and scrape downwards, putting all the weight into the finish across his ankle joint. This has the effect of scraping all the skin off his shin and smashing all the small bones on the top of his foot, a very tender and unprotected part of the body. It renders the foot completely useless, and as your man topples forward finish him with an uppercut to the jaw or the knee in the crotch.

Always remember that a kick on the shins will make the strongest man lurch forward and bend in the middle— in other words, stick his chin out. Chins in this position were meant for uppercuts. If you are not sure of your punch, pull him forwards and downwards by the neck or shoulders and bring your knee up to meet his face as it comes down!

OPPONENT UNARMED

Street fighting, Home Guard fighting, will become very general if the Boche invades this island, particularly with air-borne and parachute troops, as their equipment is bound to be limited at first. Further, there will be many opportunities, particularly in your own town, of catching him around a corner, and it is here that hand-to-hand work will be of the utmost importance. Here again let us emphasize the importance of surprise and speed.

It was said of Lord Trenchard, the great father of the Royal Air Force, that he made many decisions, fifty per cent. of them wrong, but he made them so fast and carried them out with such vigour that the mistakes were almost never noticed. Remember that the German is a stranger in your town; with all the organization in the world he cannot know his way around like you do. Particularly in the early phases of an action his knowledge and morale will be at their lowest: every minute spent on your ground makes him more sure of himself and his surroundings. Personally, I always like to keep a saying of the great Lord Nelson's in mind: "*I am convinced that the boldest action is always the safest.*"

First let us recognize that whether he comes at you or you go at him, the first things you are going to make contact with are his arms. Nobody starts a fight with his hands behind his back. Therefore there are only two cases worth consideration—either he grips your arms first or you grip his.

15

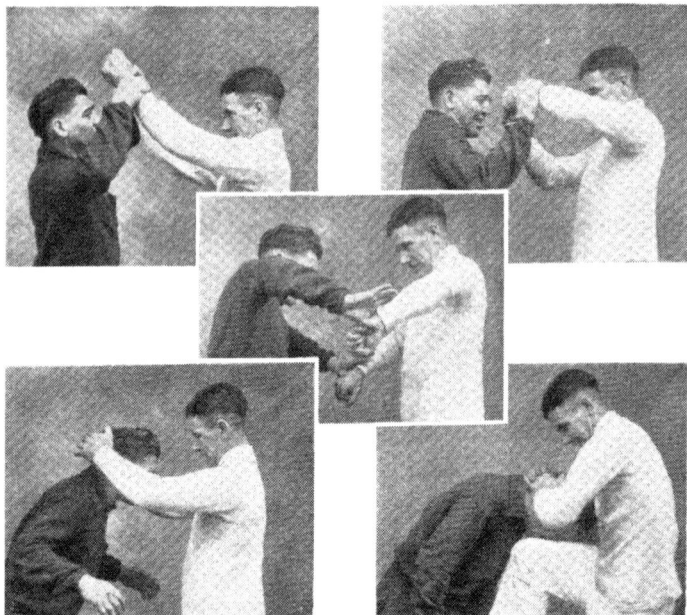

WRIST RELEASES

CLOTHING HELD

16

WRIST RELEASES

His first grasp will invariably be at your wrists or forearms. Look at the plate. He will have four fingers on one side of your arm and only his thumb on the other side. Work on the thumb. The strongest man's thumb will not be stronger than your whole arm. To achieve the maximum force and surprise, start by lifting your arms upwards; then as your man exerts force to pull them down again swing them down and out, pressing against his thumb. He will have to let go: it is impossible to hold on. By swinging down and out vigorously your arms will come free above his and his body will be jerked forward. Continue your arm swing to the back of his head and bring the knee upwards, thus smashing his face on your kneecap, stepping slightly forward as you do to ensure a large surface of contact and the maximum damage.

HAIR OR CLOTHING HELD

You will readily see from the plate that to grasp a person in this manner means a right-angular bend in the wrist to start with. In other words, a maximum bend. Bend it any more and he must either bend his whole body or let go. If done with speed he will almost invariably let go, and the chances of breaking his wrist are equally good. Hold your hands straight and rigid together, using the sharp edge to press into his wrist joint; step in close and bend forward from the shoulders, at the same time giving him your knee in the crotch. This will get you free and leave you in a position for a blow to the jaw, or smash his face against your knee.

17

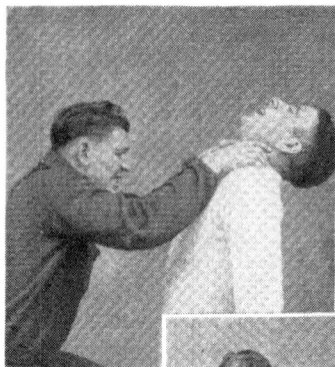

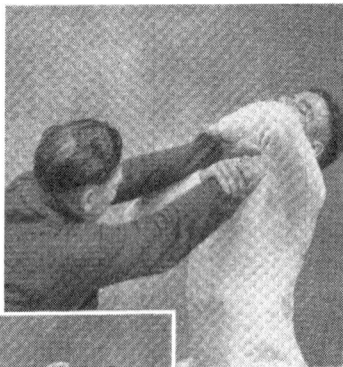

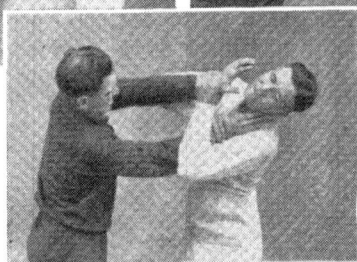

RELEASE FROM STRANGLEHOLD

18

STRANGLEHOLD

Whether from the front or behind (and get this straight, it is physically impossible for you to be throttled provided you keep your head; and it is easy to keep your head if you will realize how small is your actual danger), no man with courage or knowledge would ever use a stranglehold. It is—or should be, provided you " know your stuff "—suicide.

Once again there are only two cases worth considering —when you are fairly evenly matched, and when your man is much stronger than you are. In either case, you can easily master the situation.

The first one illustrated is always worth a try, and will only fail against a much stronger opponent, when you can switch to the second method shown.

Grasp your opponent's opposite wrists—that is, cross your hands, taking his right in yours, and his left in yours, right arm under, left arm over as shown in the plate. Push out on both his arms. This will make him force inward, which is just what you want him to do. When you feel this extra pressure, twist your body slightly to the left, pulling your own arms apart, thus crossing your opponent's arms above the elbow. Hold his left hand close to your body, bending his right arm across it. This will force your opponent off balance to his left rear. As he is falling give him your right knee in the crotch.

As stated above, this can only fail against a very strong man. In this case, go for his thumbs or little fingers, whichever you strike first, and pull them away from your throat. Once again, no man has thumbs or single fingers which are stronger than your whole arms. As you pull away kick him in the shins or crotch; and if you still feel the urge punch him in the jaw as he goes down. There are many variations of this trick. This is the easiest and most efficient. To learn others will only cause confusion.

THE FLYING MARE

20

HELD AROUND THE WAIST

As already stated, the first principle of this kind of rough-and-tumble is to keep your opponent at arm's length. The idea is simply that you want to inflict as much damage with as little done to yourself as possible. The second and only other rule to remember is **never go to the ground with your opponent.** It is obvious that this means getting close to him, and once again being close you will not have room to see what he is up to or to work yourself.

However, if you are so unfortunate as to get caught around the waist, particularly from behind, there is no need to give up the ghost. There is also no need to wriggle and struggle and try to get your arms free simply by pushing and shoving. Remember, energy is precious: do not waste it. You have already been shown how to use your helmet in such an emergency. Obviously with both arms pinned to your sides, the only other weapons you have to work with are your feet. The moment you feel yourself grasped in this manner lash out for his shins, and/or give him your knee in his crotch : he is very vulnerable to both these forms of attack, and does not know his job or he would not have attacked you in this fashion. This will make him loosen his grip and give you a chance to get your arms free, whereupon you can apply a punch or an arm lock—as shown elsewhere in this pamphlet.

ARM LOCKS

This brings us to the case where you grasp the Boche first. Once again, there are only two conditions worth considering—first when you are both relatively stationary, and, second, when he comes at you on the run.

We will concern ourselves with just two types of arm locks—the simple elbow break and the " flying mare," so well known in professional wrestling where it is responsible for some of the most spectacular falls—usually well rehearsed in advance! They both depend for their success

21

THE ELBOW BREAK

22

ARM LOCKS—(continued)

on the simple principle laid down earlier in this work, namely, that the elbow is designed to bend only one way, and if it is bent in the opposite direction it must either break or your opponent goes to the ground. This fact is responsible for those thrilling throws mentioned just now in the professional ring; the man is not actually thrown at all. Jumping over his opponent's shoulder is the only way of getting out of the grip!

THE FLYING MARE

First, the flying mare. Grasp your opponent's right wrist or forearm with both hands. Pivot quickly on the left foot, carrying his arm over your own left shoulder, so that your shoulder comes between his elbow and his shoulder, twisting his wrist to keep the palm of his hand uppermost—this is most important, otherwise he will be able to bend his elbow and the break will not work. It will readily be seen that the slightest downward pressure in this position will cause his arm to break, using your own shoulder as the fulcrum.

THE ELBOW BREAK

Next, the elbow break, which is perhaps of more use as a " come along," as a man can be kept under control without any discomfort or danger to yourself. In this you grasp your opponent's right wrist or forearm in your own right, pivot on the right foot, swinging the left to a position just beside your opponent's right foot. At the same time, throw your left arm over above his elbow, and under it again to bring your left hand back across your own body. Now by applying a downward pressure to his arm with your right hand his elbow can easily be broken across your own left arm, which is braced across your own body. To make your grip firmer, grasp your own right arm with your left hand as you are holding him.

23

THE ARM BREAK

24

ARM BREAK

This is simply a fast method of elbow breaking, for use when your man comes at you on the run. Remembering the element of surprise, make use of his own speed to bring about his downfall. As he advances stand your ground firmly. As he sets himself to charge you he unconsciously judges his distance and the exact spot where he expects to make contact. By waiting till the last possible moment and then moving slightly to the side, you throw his calculations just a few inches off and he is for an instant off balance and coming forward with a fair degree of speed. In this case we will assume that you made a turn half-left, pivoting quickly on the right foot. As he reaches you, arms outstretched to grasp you, seize his right arm with both hands. Jerk his arm forward to increase his speed and as he goes past you throw your left shoulder vigorously into his arm between his shoulder and his elbow.

" ALWAYS THE BOLDEST ACTION "

OPPONENT ARMED

It must be obvious to everyone that if you have no weapon and your opponent has one you are in a pretty sticky position. However, let me suggest this to you. He is a Hun, he is armed, you are not, his business is to kill you; either you sit back and " take it," or you put up a fight for your life. Personally, I prefer to fight; and if you have any Irish in you you will prefer to fight anyway. This brings us back to the first principle of military strategy— the element of surprise. If he is armed and you are not, the last thing he expects is for you to attack him. Therefore half your object is achieved from the start: it is only necessary once again to execute your movement with speed and vigour. Remember Lord Nelson—" always the boldest action."

You will remember that when both of you are unarmed we told you to keep your man at arm's length; when he is armed the opposite applies. The reason for this is simple enough. If you crowd him he will not have room to use his weapon, whatever it is, and also you will have a better chance of getting your hands on it when you can.

First we will consider close quarters against a man with a tommy-gun, automatic pistol or revolver. If he shoots you before you can get close to him—well, that is " one on the house," and the more fool you for not stalking him carefully. However, we are considering that you can get close to him without committing suicide. The most effective action is to half-turn the body, quickly crashing the forearm, on the appropriate side, against his weapon as near as possible to his hand. A really good blow with a hard, bony arm will usually knock the weapon completely out of his hand, and even if it does not you have decreased the size of the target and forced the gun off your own body. As you will see from the plate, it is now pointing past you and not at you, and therefore there is no immediate danger. From here apply either an arm lock or hit him on the jaw, or kick him in the place where it hurts most.

"IF HE DIGS HIS GUN IN YOUR BACK"

28

Next we will take the case where you are being taken prisoner—a most futile pastime at best; that is where the Boche has his weapon, tommy-gun or revolver, either in your back or in your stomach. First a few simple points in handling this type of weapon. Let me tell you a short story of an incident a few years ago in Chicago. A policeman was detailed to make an arrest. When he walked into the culprit's office the man snatched up a revolver and pointed it at the policeman's head. The latter walked calmly across the room, disarmed his man and arrested him. He was hailed as a hero. As he pointed out himself, he was never in any danger at all. Why? It is simple. In the first place, no one who knows how to use a revolver ever points it at your head; because all revolvers " jump," and the shot would have gone completely over his head, even if it had been fired. Second, if your man intends to shoot you he will do so at once and not give you the opportunity to turn the tables on him. In the same way, if a Hun digs his gun in your back or stomach, he obviously does not intend to shoot you—not at once, at any rate. One-tenth of a second is all you need in which to act. Look at the plate: from back or front the action is the same. When he makes you raise your hands never put them up straight; hold them as far apart as possible, then he cannot focus both arms at the same time. Once again sweep the arm down and strike his hand where he grips the weapon, half turning the body as you do so. His gun will now be pointing off your body and you will have him off guard. By this time you should know what to do next.

Practise this with an empty revolver and tell your opponent to really try to pull the trigger. The author has made it a point in all his demonstrations to ask people to come up and try to shoot him; he can honestly say that no one has ever succeeded. It takes far longer for him to " get wise " to what you are up to and to make up his mind to press the trigger than it does for you to make that simple movement with your arm; literally, this never fails. Try it with an empty gun and you will soon be convinced of the truth.

PARRYING A RIFLE AND BAYONET

PARRYING A RIFLE AND BAYONET

A bayonet is probably the toughest proposition a man can be asked to face. But, once again, you have only this simple choice: either you let Nature take its course and hope the insurance company will take care of your family or you fight for it. He obviously intends to kill you, anyway, so you might as well go down fighting; and if you learn this easy trick properly your chances of survival are remarkably good. The secret of the whole thing is that you must stand your ground to the very last possible moment, and move only when your opponent is right on top of you. That takes guts, true, but if you don't the Boche will take a good deal more.

As your opponent comes at you, parry the rifle to your left with your left forearm, and grasp his leading hand firmly with your left hand. Pivot the body half-left from the left foot, and seize his left arm just below the shoulder. Hold with the left hand and press down with the right; as your man bends kick him violently with your right knee on his rear end. He must either go down or drop his rifle. This leaves him bent double with his back to you and you holding the rifle; transfer the right hand to the rifle and smash the butt into his head.

31

PARRYING A KNIFE

PARRYING A KNIFE

It is not perhaps generally realized that all German soldiers and sailors carry knives, and are taught how to use them. Once again you are undoubtedly in a spot; and the only successful action must be taken from a firm stand: if you raise your arm to parry the blow while your opponent is still ten feet away from you, it will be an easy matter for him to change his direction and foil you. You must wait till the last possible moment before you act. As he comes to strike, raise your left forearm horizontally across your face, catching his forearm across yours. Swing the right arm under his right between his elbow and his shoulder. Clasp your hands together and press to his right rear—that is your left front—at the same time giving him your right knee in the crotch. This is another version of the elbow break, and he must go down; you have your whole weight and both arms concentrated against his right forearm.

The action is very similar for the odd case in which your assailant uses an understroke rather than an overstroke. The forearm parry is exactly the same except that you parry low rather than high, as shown in the plate. From here an arm lock can be very simply applied with the desired results.

33

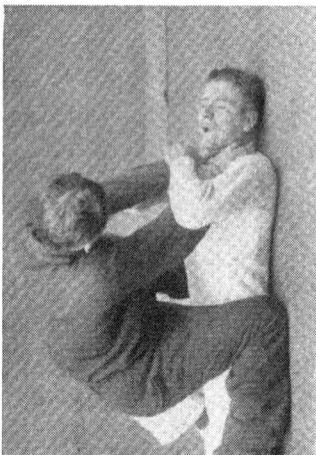

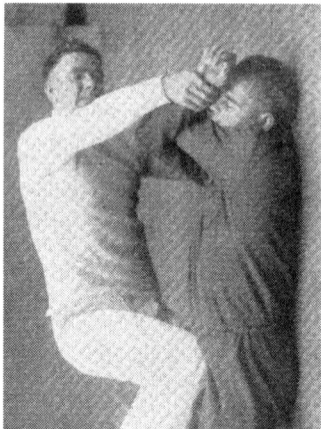

"DON'T WASTE TIME OR ENERGY ON THE GROUND"

GROUND WORK

You have already been told never to go to the ground with a man; however, accidents happen in the best-regulated families, so it may even happen that you are attacked while you are sleeping, or otherwise lying on the ground. Here again there are only two alternatives worth considering. Your man will either try to throttle you or hit you in the face. In either case, his arms will be in front of your face and easily reached for an arm lock, which, combined with a twist of the body, will reverse your positions. The arm lock is applied exactly as for the stranglehold in the standing position. He will obviously have both arms in the fray, and therefore you have two arms to work on.

As you cross his arms as already taught, vigorously twist the body and throw upwards with your hips. This will throw the man off you, and the twisting of his arms will put you on top. As mentioned in the beginning, when you have a man in this position do not waste time and energy in either of the futile pursuits of hitting or strangling. Grab his hair, his ears or just his head in general, and smash it recklessly on the ground.

"GET HIM UNDER CONTROL WITHOUT A SOUND"

STALKING A SENTRY

This is simply a combination of things already taught, and there are many versions of it; the only one given here is without doubt the most effective and easy to learn; do not confuse your mind with alternatives.

In stalking a man from behind, your object is to get him under control without a sound; and that means preventing him from crying out when he is seized. You will remember that the base of the spine is a very vulnerable nerve centre, and that a well-delivered punch here causes a temporary black-out. First hit your sentry a hard punch with the right hand in the small of the back; the German soldier does not carry any equipment covering this part of the body. At the same time swing the left arm across his throat, keeping the hand and fingers extended, thumb inwards. This gives you a sharp rather than a rounded edge next his throat and is much more painful. Next bring the right arm up to the back of his neck, securing your left hand in your own right elbow joint. Once again keep the hand extended with the sharp edge of the forearm against his neck. It will now be seen that his neck is secured firmly between your two arms and you have perfect leverage to apply the pressure. If you intend to take him alive do not put too much pressure on his neck, because in this position it can be broken very easily.

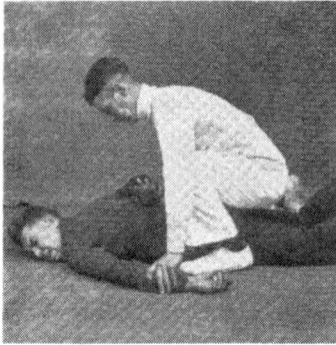

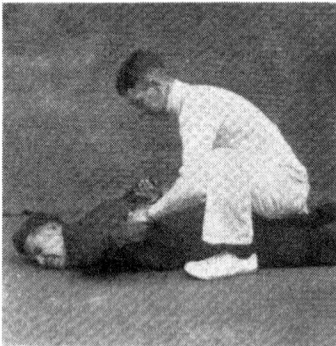

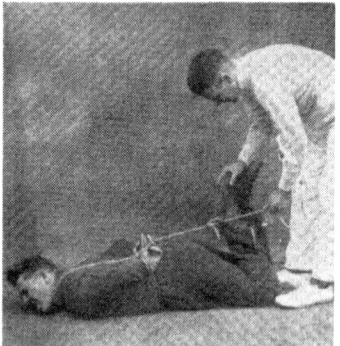

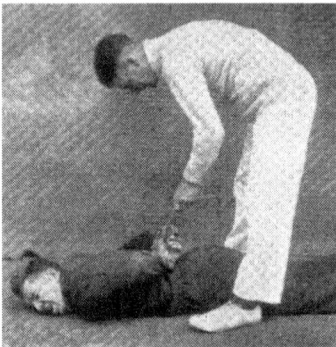

"THERE IS NO POSSIBLE WAY OUT OF THIS"

TYING A PRISONER

This can be simply carried out from any arm lock, and is easy to execute, because with the pressure you can apply it is very simple to get your victim's co-operation.

Force his hand up the middle of his back; try it on a friend and you will find that he will readily do everything you demand of him. Make him put up his other hand and tie them tightly together, bent up double in between his shoulder-blades. Next bend his knees back and tie his feet similarly. Now secure a cord to his knotted wrists, pass it around his throat and down his back to his feet, which you have tied, likewise behind his back. If he struggles at all or tries to loosen his hands or feet he will simply succeed in strangling himself! There is no possible way out of this.